by John and Gary Millea

The Beatles

The Beatles are the biggest selling and most popular band in history. Here's the story of four young boys and their rise to stardom.

over
2 BILLION
records sold!

John Lennon
October 9, 1940

(James) Paul McCartney
June 18, 1942

Once upon a time, in the industrial English port town of Liverpool, four future stars were born.

George Harrison
February 25, 1943

Richard Starkey
(Ringo Starr)
July 7, 1940

John started a band called The Quarrymen,

John asked Paul to join,

Paul asked George to join, shortly after which they changed the band's name to first Johnny and the Moondogs and then The Silver Beetles

and finally Ringo was asked to join the band, now called The Beatles (with an 'A').

Elvis Presley

Fats Domino

Woolton Parish Church

Garden Fete

and

Crowning of Rose Queen

Saturday, July 6th, 1957

PROCESSION AT 2PM

LIVERPOOL POLICE DOGS DISPLAY
FANCY DRESS PARADE
THE QUARRY MEN SKIFFLE GROUP
Adults 6d., Children 3d.

GRAND DANCE

at 8p.m. in the Church Hall

GEORGE EDWARDS' BAND
THE QUARRY MEN SKIFFLE GROUP

Tickets 2/-

Leach Entertainments Invites you to

'A NIGHT TO REMEMBER'

TOWER BALLROOM
NEW BRIGHTON

FRIDAY 6TH APRIL
7.30P.M. - 1A.M

EMILE FORD
AND THE CHECKMATES
WITH
THE BEETLES

(THEIR FAREWELL PERFORMANCE PRIOR TO A TWO MONTHS SEASON IN GERMANY)

Tickets 6'

PARAMOUNT'S
21
PLUS NIGHT

WHIT MONDAY
6th June

GROSVENOR BALLROOM

THE BIG BEAT BOYS! 2 STAR BANDS
Direct from their tour with Johnny Gentle
THE FABULOUS SILVER BEATLES
also
GERRY & THE PACE-MAKERS

BEEKAY presents

JIVE AT LATHOM HALL
Every SATURDAY

THIS WEEK
SILVER BEATS, DOMINOES, DELTONES

7:30 — 11:30   Admission 4/-. Memebers 3/6

MERSEYSIDE CIVIL SERVICE CLUB

THE FABULOUS BEATLES

On Tuesday, 7th November, 1961

Guest's Ticket 3/-

The member whose name appears on the reverse of this ticket must accompany the bearer and sign the Visitor's Book at the time of admission

In the early days the band practiced and performed anywhere they could, from Liverpool to Hamburg, they played in living rooms, doorways, bars, buses, churches, schools and cafes.

'Swinging Lunch Time Rock Sessions'

LIVERPOOL JAZZ SOCIETY

Next Wednesday Afternoon

March 15th, 1961
12-00 to 5-00 Special

STARRING —
**The Beatles,
Gerry and the Pacemakers
Rory Storm and the Wild Ones**

Admisson — Members 1/-, Vistors 1/6

"Rocking at the L.S.J."

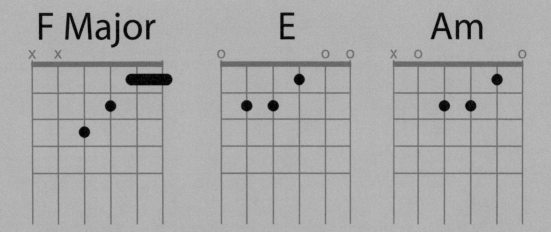

Like many of their heroes, John, Paul and George loved to play the guitar and spent hours and hours practicing.

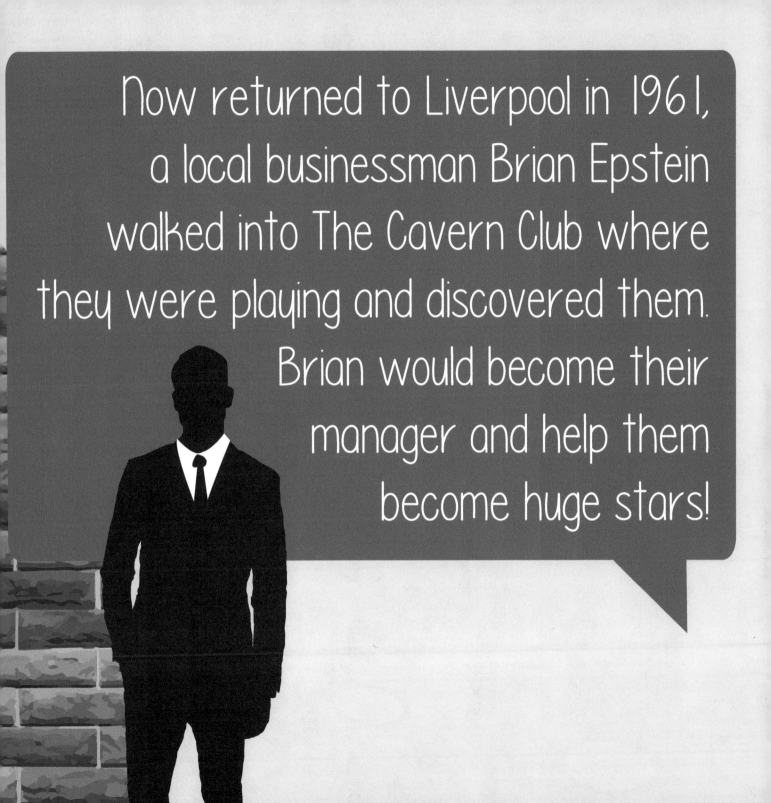

Parlophone

Love Me Do
(Lennon-McCartney)
THE BEATLES

After much trying, Brian got them a record deal with Parlophone Records and George Martin, who would be their producer for their entire career.

Nearly all The Beatles music was recorded at Abbey Road Studios, in the heart of London.

ABBEY ROAD

N.W.8

CITY OF WESTMINSTER

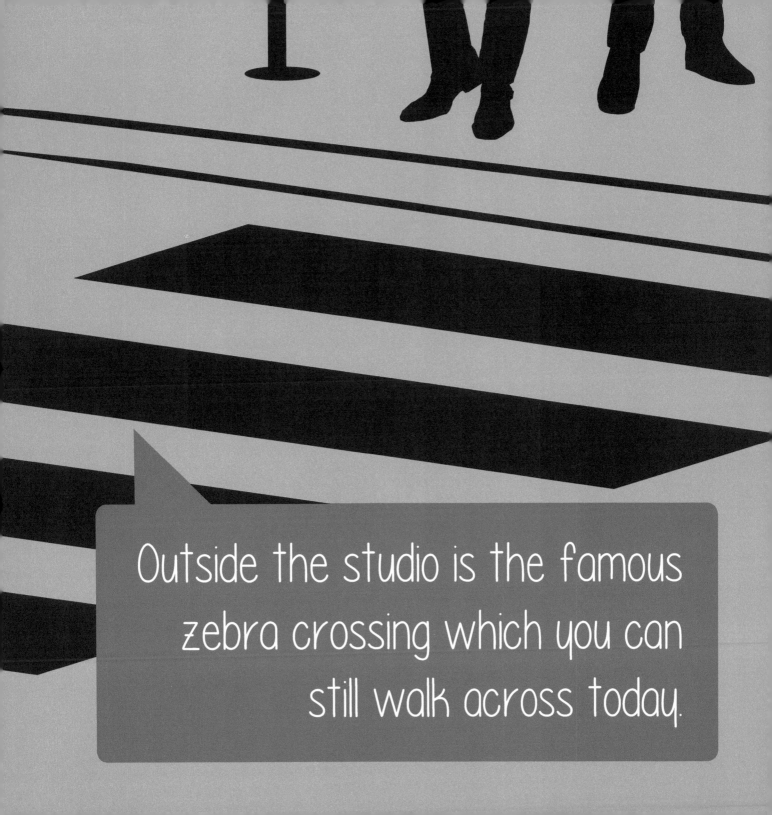

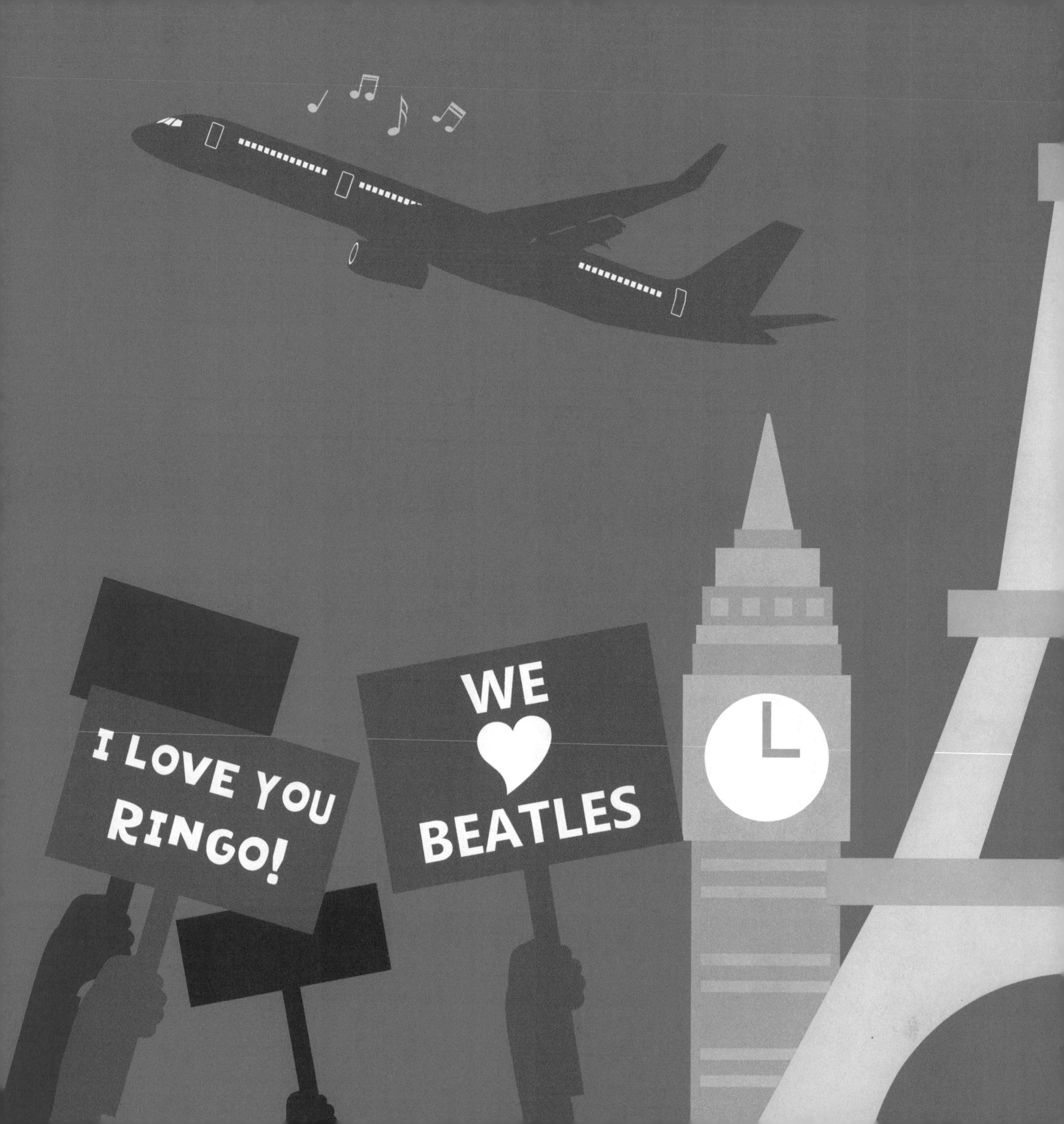
I LOVE YOU
RINGO!
WE
BEATLES

They made many hit records and became huge stars in the United Kingdom and Europe. Beatlemania was spreading, but the biggest was yet to come...

On February 7, 1964, they landed in New York to a screaming crowd. After playing to a TV audience of 73 million people on the Ed Sullivan Show, America fell in love with them.

Over the next few years, while still making hit records and films, they played hundreds of concerts in over a hundred different cities around the world.

In 1966, tired of playing concerts and traveling, they went into the record studio and emerged a few months later with their greatest masterpiece.

In 1967, the Summer of Love, The Beatles recorded the song 'All You Need is Love' and played it to a TV audience of over 500 million people.

The Beatles continued to record and release albums until April 1970. Eight years after their first record, they split up.

Need
Lovely
Universe
Everywhere
Good
Dance
Girl
Ive
Loving
You
Lady
Sun
Someone
Sky
Hey
Im
Love
Want
Hearts
Dear
Life
Her
Natures
Slumbers
She
Love
Please
Honey
Sleeping
Yeah
Need
Penny
Naturally

In the end, their songs remain in our lives, hearts and souls, with their universal themes of peace, love and understanding.

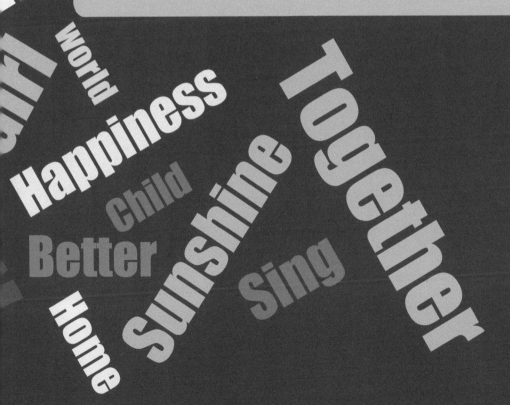

CPSIA information can be obtained
at www.ICGtesting.com
Printed in the USA
LVHW071701130919
630970LV00005B/131/P

9 780692 986530